— INSPIRED B

Frida

JOURNAL

AKAL PRITAM

ROCKPOOL

Make a journal of your creative destiny. a very beautiful, intricate picture of your dreams.

Considered to be one of Mexico's greatest
artists, Frida Kahlo began painting mostly
self-portraits after she was severely injured
in a bus accident, using her artistic voice with
courage and purpose.
The strength and power of Frida Khalo's
creative spirit has left a legacy that
inspires unapologetic self-expression
and celebrates the potential to overcome
great challenges.
Frida's legacy reminds us all of the value of being
a truly creative individual beyond any self-limitation.
Work through this journal to overcome
any blocks and fears that prevent you
realising your full creative potential,
consistently uplifting yourself to
fulfil your dharma.
Be ready for miracles to happen as you work to
open yourself to courageously explore
and express your highest creative potential.

freedom

you are always free
to love, to be creative,
to give with all your
beautiful heart. ♡

Do you know your soul?

You are free; do you feel this? What does this mean to you?

Say: 'I am free. I am free. I am free.'

It's your birthright to explore your creative path and be happy your entire life.

Go to the depth of your heart, speak with who you are and know yourself intimately.

I am free to dream . . .

Choose to see creative energy in everything no matter what and you will recognise opportunity.

The 13 ghosts
that are dancing
in your mind
are waiting for
your heart to
set them free.
They are thorny
old voices,
perceiving
only loss
when soft
petals fall.
Yet in the
strong heart
stories of woe
are fragrantly
retold with
fondness,
gratitude,
knowing,
forgiveness,
compassion,
understanding,
wisdom,
acceptance,
humour,
hope,
faith,
trust and
love.

With reverence,
self-reverence,
nothing is excluded;
everything about you
is included,
named
or yet to be named.
In the heart,
held tenderly,
ever so lightly,
with breathing space,
crying space,
laughing like an idiot
space to be
a muse and amusing.
Observed,
studied,
a true beloved,
loved in every
aspect,
every perspective;
a sacred subject
for expression in
a painting,
a song,
a poem,
a bowl of soup,
ten stitches on a blouse,
a room with
cushions, an altar and a view.

Reverence

Catch your burning soul;
place poetry in your mind,
a candle in your heart,
flowers in your hair

What is your intent?

To what do you consent?

You can only lift others above fear with creativity, love and a lightness of being.

You belong to life. With love and reverence you will find the peace and harmony of this.

Dress yourself with reverence. Bow to the infinite within you and radiate that.

I am invaluable in every aspect: INVALUABLE!

Your life has magnitude; you are magnificent. Honour yourself with a grateful attitude.

It is the opportunity,
the birthright,
the calling of
every woman to
hold reverence for
human potential
and believe in the
success, evolution and
refinement of every
individual.
Women are made to birth the future,
courageously dreaming and
envisioning new
expressions of the
creative life force.
Woman is the
salve for any social
rendition of apathy
and stagnancy, of 'couldn't, wouldn't,
shouldn't'.
Woman is given
immense divine energy
to use to confidently
create, not to control.
Woman is a flower,
who upon releasing her unique
fragrance to
the aching world
propels life to go on.

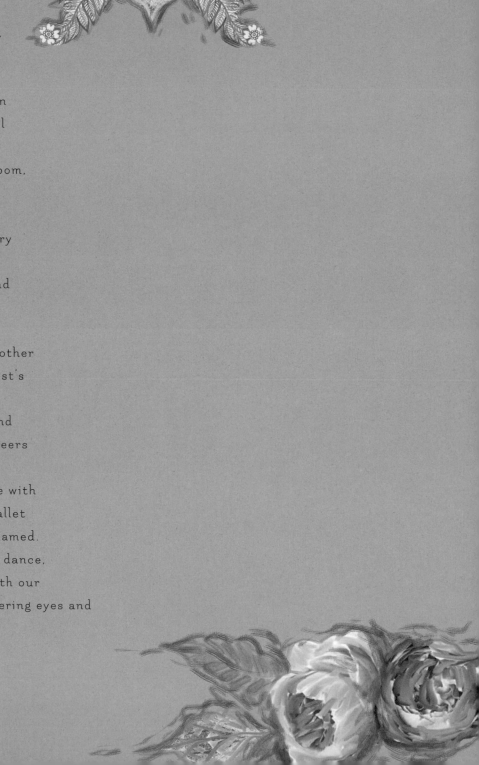

We are the bridges
of the language of heart,
the genius of art
embodied in softness,
fullness, fluidity.
Every step with feet
on the ground, head in
the clouds, we are tall
and unique, warriors
of love, of infinite bloom,
the torch bearers for
what hasn't been,
weaving a rich tapestry
in a co-continuum.
We know of no end and
are always and only
just beginning, eager
and inspired by each other
and the immortal artist's
fragrance lingering.
We breathe and expand
into new beauty, pioneers
of the art of heart,
the art of making love with
life itself, mixing a pallet
of colours yet to be named.
We paint, we sing, we dance,
we dress our souls with our
golden laughter, glittering eyes and
unapologetically wear
flowers in our hair.

Inspired

Touch the world with the light of your soul, by living in spirit.

What are you waiting for?

Self belief is a choice.
Belief opens doors.

A soul that touches the world with its truest creativity will leave a legacy of love.

Don't play wishy-washy. Paint the world with your clarity, and create with clear ideas about love.

Don't play small, don't pretend to be shy: that's a child's game. Play with the joy that is inside of you; play with wonder and magic.

Allow the wellspring of your true self to fill you. Be full of yourself, and choose to embody success as it's your birthright.

You're a living work of art; you're always becoming your true self.

Dive into your life; let your beautiful words and actions become inspirational.

Frida inspires us
to remember our soul's
infinite potential,
our divine name,
our creative flame.
We can each live
as creative spirit
liberated from
conclusion,
a fragrance that
beckons hearts
out of darkness.
Fear dies;
only love lives on.
Each unique essence
of soul creativity,
purified and embodied
through the alembic
of the artist's heart,
becomes a sacred
ray of hope.
When a soul walks
this earth leaving
a lasting legacy
of creativity,
this memory flows
through the roots
of all the trees,
the songs of birds,
through the
wind and rain,
flowers and clay.

Could you be devoted to the
task of truly loving yourself?
Could you pledge to create an
opening in your heart for
yourself that you never close?
The inextinguishable,
brilliant flame of love that
burns with hope and courage is
within you to realise the new,
to joyously be an
unfinished work of art,
willing to share and make
beautiful connections.
Self-devotion isn't about
being perfect or reaching a
conclusion; it's about making a
commitment self to self
to surrender to the journey of
the soul.

self devoted

Devotion

Surrender to the creative journey of the soul, the flame of love.

enjoy every breath

I walk playfully.

Give the world hope with your warm smile, effective etiquette and graceful heart.

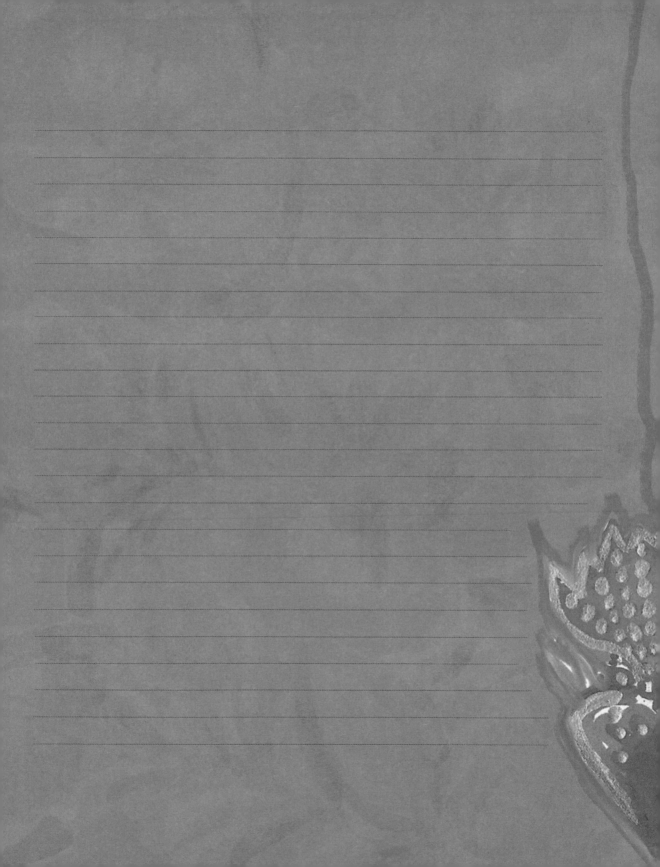

Apply your gifts to life, and work hard in your own direction so you can feel contentment.

make a

_____

_____

_____

_____

_____

_____

_____

_____

_____

_____

_____

_____

_____

_____

_____

_____

_____

_____

_____

_____

_____

Your endurance will bring you success. Never defend yourself, remain present in your heart.

Be prepared for more learning, more understanding, more opportunities and more love.

Devoted.
Endless.
Deathless.
Flame of love.
Valiant gratitude.
Beyond words.
Courageous will.
Boundless hope.
No words can say
what the heart
is capable of.
Tested again
and again
and again.
Allegiance.
Infinite journey
of the soul.
Love.
Devotion.

amour

self devoted

I accept.
I do.
I accept
I am gifted.
I really do.
And I trust
these gifts
are granted
to give
forth freely.
I agree to
embrace my
natural-born
talents so that
I may fulfil
my beautiful
creative destiny.

Acceptance

I accept I have gifts and a beautiful, unique creative destiny

I am supported.

I am loved

Don't miss the best, most creative opportunity because it looks like work.

Hard work is happiness.

Don't be afraid of the biggest unknown in your life: your potential. It's a gift, so unwrap it each day.

Let your creativity take you between nothing and everything. Your heart knows the way.

Scatter the seeds of your wild and tender dreams with your singing fingers.

Your dreams won't expire. Keep believing, and never, ever give up on yourself.

I accept the responsibility of
listening to my heart and soul,
courageously taking action to
creatively express my truth.
I am the only one who knows
what will fulfil my creative
purpose. I accept I am unique
and I celebrate all that I am.
I have been given the gift of
this miraculous life for the
purpose of making love real.
I love who I am.